SELECTED POEMS
1970-1985

TONY CURTIS
SELECTED POEMS
1970–1985

*For Elaine
with warmest of wishes
at Edinburgh.*

POETRY WALES PRESS
1986

July 86

POETRY WALES PRESS
56 PARCAU AVENUE, BRIDGEND, MID GLAMORGAN

British Library Cataloguing in Publication Data
Curtis, Tony, *1946-*
   Selected poems, 1970-1985.
   I. Title
   821'.914   PR6053.U1

ISBN 0-907476-59-7

The publisher acknowledges the financial support of the
Welsh Arts Council

Cover painting: Motorway Journey by Alan Salisbury
Cover design by Jeane Rees

Typeset by Wordsmiths Ltd.
Printed in 10 point Plantin
by Antony Rowe Ltd.

CONTENTS

NEW POEMS

from WALK DOWN A WELSH WIND

from ALBUM

THE DEERSLAYERS

from PREPARATIONS

from LETTING GO

Acknowledgements

English, *The Listener*, *Stand*, *The Mississippi Valley Review*, *The Dalhousie Review*, *The South Dakota Review*, *The Malahat Review*, *The Anglo-Welsh Review*, *Poetry Wales*, *Poetry Review*, *Kayak*, *Outposts*, *2 Plus 2*, *Keltica*, *Poetry Canada Review*, *Poetry Durham*, *Confrontation*, *The Observer*, *Stand*, *The Kenyon Review*, *The Reaper*, *The Jewish Chronicle Literary Supplement*, *Word and Image*.

Anglo-Welsh Poetry 1480-1980 (Poetry Wales Press), *Wales in Verse* (Secker & Warburg), *Green Horse* (Christopher Davies), *The Carmarthenshire Anthology* (Christopher Davies), *Anthology of American Magazine Verse, 1980* (Monitor Book Co.).

BBC Radio 3, BBC Radio 4, BBC Radio Wales, the University of Missouri *New Letters on the Air* cassette series, *Wales – Landscape and Legend*, Channel 4 television, Skopje television, Yugoslavia.

'Land Army Photographs', 'Tannenbaum' and 'Ivy' first appeared in *The New Yorker*.

'Jack Watts' won the Stroud Festival Prize, 1980, and 'Affairs' that prize in 1981.

'Crane-flies' was a runner-up in the National Poetry Competition, 1982, and 'The Death of Richard Beattie-Seaman in the Belgian Grand Prix, 1939' won the National Poetry Competition in 1984.

'Worm' won the Basil Bunting Prize in 1985.

'Ivy' was a runner-up for the Greenwich Festival Prize.

These poems are selected from:

Walk Down a Welsh Wind (Phoenix Pamphlet Series, 1972)
Album (Christopher Davies, 1974)
Three Young Anglo-Welsh Poets (Welsh Arts Council, 1974)
The Deerslayers (Cwm Nedd Press, 1977)
Preparations (Gomer Press, 1980)
Letting Go (Poetry Wales Press, 1983)

NEW POEMS

Taken to the Sea

This last one came to poetry late
and read outwards in hungry circles
– Dylan, Rilke, Yeats and Blake –
searching for the voices that sustain.

As my mother lately
has taken to the sea
in a borrowed costume
risking more and more to the water

who had rarely dipped an ankle in her life
so that each wave now laps and wrinkles
more of her. A winter
in the pool will see her float

loosen into the element until it holds her.
The sea receives us without struggle
if we let ourselves fall.
Next summer she'll dive at Skrinkle

five years and two beaches around
from where we cast my father's urn, shaken empty
then flooding full in those August waves.
This last one came late to poetry.

Two for Luck

The morning started badly –
A thin frost, damp on the plugs,

One magpie rising off the railway crossing
As the gates rattled shut for the Sunday milk crawler.

The car-park jammed full at the club.
Driven pegs snapping on the first tee.

Then on the seventh fairway,
At the top of his backswing,

The knife pushed out of his chest
And somehow he knew what to do –

Lowered his iron and walked in
To the clubhouse with an "Excuse me."

Drove steadily home and said quite firmly:
"Phone for Henderson at the surgery,

And an ambulance, I'm going to have
An attack."

"But ... why ... ?"
"Give me air," he said,

And walked out on the patio
Measuring his pace, avoiding the cracks.

Opaquely through a lifting haze, the sun glowed
On the new leaves, the tight crowns of apple-blossom.

He stooped to pull a weed
And caught the smell of earth.

He stood there until they arrived to lay
Him between the red blankets, knees drawing

Up to the foetal position, one hand
In his wife's hand, the other

Fisting at his chest and
The blades working like beaks

Against the breast-cage, all the way
As they sirened across town

To the bed where the mask closed over him.
They said – "Sleep."

And he dreamed of that approach like a bullet,
The ball biting and holding up to the lip of the cup,

His long walk across the green
To lift aloft the pin flying the black

And white body of a dead magpie
Its wing-feathers edged with the sharpest blue.

Field of Wheat

Out from the storming night they came
and before them the field bowed
over to the sky and fell towards the sea.
Rich and gold, the wheat settled like hair
though the facing slope was shadowed at its centre.

> *See how the wheat is broken and flattened there*
> *she said – that must have been the storm.*
> *But then, why just at that point?*

He said – *that's a fox after a hare,*
some hunted creature flushed from cover.

> *No! I want an older spirit,*
> *Branwen, daughter of Llŷr, escaped from Ireland*
> *and running across a Welsh field.*

He turned back into the room – *some freak*
of wind, some current eddying down.
This room's a mess. Let's tidy up.

> *No wind's scythe, but two lovers thrashing*
> *in the field – she said*
> *as we have done.*

He shook down the quilt with peacocks
– *Stay close to me in my life, you*
and your imagination.

From the City that Shone

The thing we dreamt of most was a bath:
so we crossed the wire and made for Gonnelieu
where, it was said, a tin bath lay abandoned
near the well of the convent school.
We kept to ruined shadows down the street,
towels and soap in our haversacks.

John had a canvas bucket and filled it from the well.
The bath held firm, the water cold and sweet.
I lorded it there in the weedy garden
amidst the ransacked books strewn all about,
broken glass wicked in the sun,
then towelled dry while
John tipped the water across the grass.

I drew fresh water for him and passed the soap.
"I always sing," he said.
"Too risky."
But he splashed and hummed
– *And who shall kiss her ruby lips*
When I am far away? –

I sat on the path, my hair drying,
my head thrown back to the clearing sky
where a Taube stuttered through clouds from the West.
In those moments before the guns started up
it seemed that summer was held in place.

John rose from the water
"Like a god," he said,
his arms outstretched, then lobbed the soap
grenade-like at my head.
It squirted past me, diving in the slips.

We dressed
– each stuck a dog-rose in his tunic –
and turned back to our trenches.
Pressed into the shadows, I thought:
What does all this mean?

Two young soldiers, for a moment
Sunday-school clean in all this mess.
The Taube crossed overhead, coughing smoke,
and made desperate way to his own lines.

William Orpen & Yvonne Aubicq in the Rue Dannon

This morning he wakes early –
sun and the sounds of carts in the streets
coming through the roughly-drawn curtains,
a fine March light over the city.
She has lain an arm across his shoulder.
In sleep her beauty is muted, held somewhere
ringing like the glint of a far-off bell.
He has seen them in ruins, the churches,
the chateaux, the empty, crumbling town squares.
He has coloured them green against brown,
yellow against dirt, the torn bodies,
the green limbs under shell-hole water.
He dreamt of lobsters moving behind glass
in the restaurant at the Savoy.
Yvonne stirs under his breath,
her sleeping face turns halfway to his.
The head is perfect under night-tousled hair,
her eyelids shimmer like butterflies' wings.
There is painting and life and death.
The mayor's beautiful daughter lies in his bed.
He is having a good war.

Last August baked the mud of the Somme
into a pure, dazzling white. And there
were daisies, blood-red poppies
and a blue flower, for miles it seemed,
great masses of blue that were,
close-to, particular delicacies.
The sky a pure, dark blue and the whole air
for thirty feet up or more quivered
with white butterflies. I brushed them – I was gentle – from
my uniform as I returned to the car.
We drove on through fields of white crosses,

the butterflies slamming against my driver's glass,
as if those crosses lurched out of the unsettled earth.

At Thiepval I began to paint a trench.
It held the remnants of two soldiers
– one German, one of ours.
I could not hold the sight for too long at a time
so gave myself rest against the torn trunk of a tree.
Three sessions, an hour passed, and then
a loose shell came over and burst.
I was blown backwards head over arse.
My heavy portrait easel took the force
– a skull smashed up through the canvas –
and the whole scene was blown to hell.

He slips away from her embrace
and she murmurs in sleep.
Tomorrow or the next day it will be complete –
the light on that slope of her left shoulder,
more work on the hair perhaps. He'll
watch her comb it as he loads his palette.
He has caught her classically
holding herself back from one's gaze,
arms crossed over her breasts
pulling her robe to her right shoulder.
That teasing look will devastate.

He rises, wraps the robe about himself
and crosses to the window to light a cigarette.
From the balcony he blows smoke over Paris.

At the end of the Rue Dannon is a square.
This is where they will march her – yes
I'll say she is a spy – call her Frida Neiter –

a spy for the Boche that the French will shoot.
She does not scream or struggle,
but walks upright, across the road
to the wall.
As the soldiers raise their rifles and
the officer his sword, she lets
slip her fur coat to the ground.
Naked she stands to face them,
her arms held out from her sides.

It seems a lifetime before they fire.

The Last Candles

The final stage of our journey over
we reached Odessa. So glorious
a scene I think my eyes had never taken in –
the harbour bristling with ships of all the allied nations.
We were received at the consulate by a young man,
fresh and clean in a crisp English suit.
Courteous and gentlemanly. I had not seen
such a man for four years.

In the hotel that night my dreams were of uniforms
and wounds, but one wound served for many –
thus, a severed arm at Biyech, the lacerated
stomach of a boy in Khutanova, the bloody head
of a captured Turk in Noscov – and then swabs
fell like the first snows of Winter,
the land chill and beyond pain
under its bandages.

For breakfast we were offered good bread and an egg.
The smell of coffee made me dizzy.

At nine we leave for the harbour. The streets
packed with aimless crowds, though everything
makes way for the *Bolsheviki* in their lorries.
At the harbour gates a man of no apparent rank
holds our papers for an hour.
He has a rifle and a long knife hangs
from his belt. A red band has been clumsily
sewn to the sleeve of his coat.

Some of the Norwegian crew speak English.
My cabin proves small, but warm.
After years under canvas, sheltering in ruins,
nursing beneath shattered roofs,
I am glad to call it home.

Though the place is strange and metallic
after stone and wood and earth.

Doctor Rakhil calls to take me on deck
for our departure.
                      Ten years of living in this great land
have brought me to love it.
Though three of those years have been spent in war,
and then this anarchy, this revolution.
I see Odessa under red flags
as we cast off and the engines churn.
I feel everything moving away from me
as if Russia were a carpet being rolled to the sky.
At the harbour mouth Doctor Rakhil
gently turns me from the rail,
but is not quite quick enough.

That night, the sea pressing around me,
I dream of three things –
                      a day
in Moscow, when Nadya and I
were close enough to reach out and touch
the Tsar, and an old peasant
who had crawled through the crowd, between
the legs of the guards, clutching
his ragged petition,
still calling out as their boots struck him.
Nicholas II, Tsar of all the Russias, flickered
his eyes, but his step was the unfaltering
step of a god.
                My first dead man
in the training ward. Grey and small in the candlelight,
his mouth like a closed purse and what seemed
to be butterflies on his face. Two sugarlumps
to weigh down his eye-lids.

And at last, this leaving
Odessa. How in the shadows I saw them –
officers from the front fleeing the chaos of desertion
and caught by the Reds at the port.
They bound their feet to heavy stones
and planted them in the harbour. Swaying, grey shapes
I glimpsed from the rail, as if
bowing to me.
The last candles of my Russia
guttering and going out under the black sea.

The Death of Richard Beattie-Seaman in the Belgian Grand Prix, 1939

Trapped in the wreckage by his broken arm
he watched the flames flower from the front end.
So much pain – *Holy Jesus, let them get to me* –
so much pain he heard his screams like music
when he closed his eyes – the school organ at Rugby
Matins with light slanting down
hot and heady from the summer's high windows.
Pain – his trousers welded by flame to his legs.
His left hand tore off the clouded goggles –
rain falling like light into the heavy trees,
the track polished like a blade.
They would get to him, they were all coming
all running across the grass, he knew.

The fumes of a tuned Mercedes smelt like
boot polish and tear gas – coughing, his screams rising
high out of the cockpit – high
away back to *'38 Die Nurburgring.*
He flew in with Clara
banking and turning the Wessex through a slow circle
over the scene – sunlight flashing off the line of cars,
people waving, hoardings and loudspeakers, swastikas
and the flags of nations lifted in the wind he stirred.
She held his arm tightly, her eyes were closed.
He felt strong like the stretched wing of a bird,
the course mapped out below him.
That day Lang and Von Brauchitsch and Caracciola
all dropped out and he did it – won
in the fourth Mercedes before a crowd of half a million
– the champagne cup, the wreath around his neck,
An Englishman the toast of Germany
The camera caught him giving a Hitlergruss.

Waving arms, shouts and faces, a mosaic
laid up to this moment – La Source – tight – the hairpin
the trees – tight – La Source – keeping up the pace
Belgium – La Source hairpin too tight.

With the fire dying, the pain dying
the voices blurred beneath the cool licks of rain.
To be laid under the cool sheets of rain.
A quiet with, just perceptible, engines roaring
as at the start of a great race.

Lessons

Right up the edge of the pit
The Professor of History taught:

Every tree, every cry
Every tear, every leaf
Each death, each blade
Of grass. Remember everything!
We are scribes – one of us
Perhaps will survive
And be all our future.

The wet, black earth on our feet.
The rattle of bullets in the trees.
The sun jewelling that belt-buckle.

*

At Birkenau I saw one of your kind –
He was in the Sonderkommando at the crematoria
Scribbling lists by the light of the furnaces.
I snapped the pencil and tore the paper –
He said nothing.
We made him throw open the doors and put them in –
He was silent.
Then we shot him and fed him to the flames.
On my walk back to the barracks
I read his name in the sky.

Soup

One night our block leader set a competition:
two bowls of soup to the best teller of a tale.
That whole evening the hut filled with words –
tales from the old countries
of wolves and children
potions and love-sick herders
stupid woodsmen and crafty villagers.
Apple-blossom snowed from blue skies,
orphans discovered themselves royal.
Tales of greed and heroes and cunning survival,
soldiers of the Empires, the Church, the Reich.

And when they turned to me
I could not speak,
sunk in the horror of that place,
my throat a corridor of bones, my eyes
and nostrils clogged with self-pity.
"Speak," they said, "everyone has a story to tell."
And so I closed my eyes and said:
I have no hunger for your bowls of soup, you see
I have just risen from the Shabbat meal –
my father has filled our glasses with wine,
bread has been broken, the maid has served fish.
Grandfather has sung, tears in his eyes, the old songs.
My mother holds her glass by the stem, lifts
it to her mouth, the red glow reflecting on her throat.
I go to her side and she kisses me for bed.
My grandfather's kiss is rough and soft like an apricot.
The sheets on my bed are crisp and flat
like the leaves of a book ...

I carried my prizes back to my bunk: one bowl
I hid, the other I stirred
and smelt a long time, so long
that it filled the cauldron of my head,
drowning a family of memories.

Boxes

for Jenkin Williams

My train draws its way across England
through the stations of the harvest –
box-acres of grass rising lush and green
after this year's rainy June,
hay swathed into shapes that match the sea's
slow, summer waves in July.
And now, a half-cut field with lines,
geometric curves and parallels where tractor
or lovers have laid paths like ropes
to hold the swelling weight of summer.
The smooth wheat flanks of Gloucestershire and Wiltshire
and crops turned to stubble, with hay bales,
then, wonderfully, caught in one swirling field of rye
a mass of the brightest poppies.

Over distant London the 747s are strung like barrage
       balloons.
Now, Jenkin, I remember your story:
you flew as gunner/navigator in a Mitchell.
On such a morning in '43, six squadrons
rose from fields to the south and east
and formed over Southampton for France.
But one squadron of Dutch crews excitedly
broke radio silence and forced you all back.
So that afternoon you re-formed and once more
flew south to Cherbourg and the rocket sites.
The Germans, fore-warned, raised a box barrage
– shrapnel solid between six and eight thousand feet –
that scythed through the bombing formation.
You fused, aimed and dropped the load at speed, then
swung around, putting her nose to the coast.

A swarm of Messerschmitts tore the stragglers to pieces.
It was then your mid-gunner caught some flak –
shrapnel took half his jaw away.
You left your maps to comfort him
and held his bloody head in your lap.
A rough ride all the way back
keeping low across the sea,
and you thinking *It's not me,
Iesu Grist, poor sod, it's him, not me.*

Three days later, a clear, warm Sunday in July,
you took the long, slow train back to Wales
and his parents' home in Tredegar.
Beside you on the seat, his belongings in a tied box.
Across Berkshire, Wiltshire, all the farm counties
the fields were turning to stubble, with hay bales
and then, wonderfully, caught in one swirling field of rye
a mass of the brightest poppies.

Guard Duty

A cold spring morning in Berlin.
On the Grotewohl-Strasse the rising light reveals
no ghosts – cleaning women in head scarves flirt
with the passing soldiers. From his tower
the guard views the banalities of life in the East.
This vigilance too is banal, routine,
now no-one risks the wire, the sprint
across the seeded ground.

April 30th 1945.
Forty years on that earth-mound between the lines
is all that remains of the place.
The Unteroffizier loosens the top button of his uniform
and fingers the warmth of his throat; he imagines
that man, sallow, death-grey, his features soft as putty,
how at last he saw clearly the end of it all.
His fall was in the manner of such men of destiny:
Bonaparte wasting away the years on Elba,
pacing in a room wallpapered with arsenic roses;
months before the news escaped they'd shot the Tsar,
the Romanov family, servants, even their spaniel –
all went under the waters of an abandoned quarry;
and this last, closer defeat – *il Duce*
and his whore gunned down at Lake Como
then left to dance from streetlamps
a week in the Piazzale Loreto.

In the bunker he shot first his dogs; they'd whined
and bristled for days as the Russian thunder rolled from
       the East.
Then Eva, draining poison in the last act of her opera.
Finally, the pistol went to his head,
his nostrils catching the reek of petrol
from the cans lined along the corridor.

Like some stuffed effigy king and queen they were dragged
into the Chancellery garden, stacked on the hurried pyre.
Just a little, Aryan smoke wrote a coda to *Mein Kampf*.

Halfway through his watch, bored on this day
as any other, the guard lifts his gun
to follow a crow landing on the earth-mound.
It scissors its untidy wings and pecks away
at a worm. He snugs the Kaı..shnikov into his shoulder,
drawing the sights in line
with its bobbing head. He purses
his lips like a boy at play
knowing he could squeeze the trigger,
startle the thing into so many bloody pieces.

Lines at Barry

Morning light steely and sharp on the docks-water
and beyond, outlining a ship in the grey Channel.
At berth, one banana ship white against the old mill
      building
where, you say, a forest of masts grew in the sun,
filling your great-grandfather's vision
as he rounded Friar's Point.

Ten days rowing from Fishguard
the length of South Wales. 1898.
Your grandmother lived her first week
in that small boat as they hugged the shore,
sheltering each night where lights marked
fire and food and life.

This is not a unique story:
each dip of his creaking blades pulling
towards coal, English and the new century.

Twenty years on he was carpenter to the town,
settled and secure in his middle life.
They'd worked all night to build a platform
for the notables, under the Stars and Stripes,
the Red Dragon, the Union Jack.
The next day he took his place in the crowd
around King's Square and stretched for a view.
This is where the Yanks first came in,
eight days rolled across the ocean
then marched in columns up from the packed, grey
      harbour.
The doughboys formed in dress order,
spreading and flexing their sea-legs,
the men bound in puttees, their officers' boots glowing,
the strange, stiff-brimmed campaign hats,
lines of polished Springfields raised against the Kaiser.

And for a moment between the speeches,
the cheering, the singing and the drill,
for a moment the lines were still and erect
as those distant masts had been for a moment still,
when the only sound was the sound of the tide pulling
his tiny boat: he saw again Sarah's tired smile,
the baby pressed to her nipple and sucking,
sucking hard, as if nothing else, not even he,
existed.

As this new morning goes, the haze
lifts slowly from the Channel, unveils
the munitions ship with her red flags up
and lighters packed with shells
drawing lines of foam to the smack centre of her sides.

Three lifetimes, two wars running to this moment –
and none of this is unique, this telling,
this drawing from memory of lines
where, steely-silver, what we are now
touches everything that made us,
and is dangerous, and shines.

In McDonough County

for Fred & Nancy Jones

Waiting for you this morning
alone and chilled in the empty house
I walked out, crossing the road and ditch to the fields.
Miles of corn, October brown rising
firm out of the black earth.

As far as the sky it stretched
and what I had taken for a block of colour, a mass
of uniform growth, showed itself particular, alive –
the electric whine of crickets, their clicked-finger jumps,
a fox, a racoon, crashing through the lines.
The corn moves in the prairie breeze,
stalks and drooping leaves that scratch
and tap against each other – the whole landscape
like the flaking skin and bristles of this world.

The sky was wider than the eye could hold –
blue with a light hand of cloud below
the high streaks of jet planes.
I felt into the hanging pods
to the smooth, full barrels of maize.

Now, at uneasy midnight, I am woken
by a low, wide rumbling – lights spark
and turn out there in the blackness.
They are working through the night
to beat the threat of rain – combines
chewing down the rows, ruling the farms' geometry.
In the damp morning light their chutes
will pour rich fountains, gold atoms
splashing into the trucks.

Dakota, Nebraska, Illinois, Iowa, Ohio –
across this vast Mid-West
the grain silos rise like cased Havanas
blunt, silver missiles.
On a high-nineties August day, without warning,
you say, one explodes.

Ivy

The choking ivy we lopped and sawed and tore
and one day – yes, in a blast of anger – burned
from the old pear still clings.

As we axed and ripped the tentacles
it slacked its biceps, unclenched its fist.
I climbed and hacked while you
dragged great clumps of ivy to your bonfire.

But high in the thirty-foot summits
clogging this season's hard, sour pears
the last clutch of parched, rootless stuff
worn like a wig still weighs on the tree.

By October winds should have scattered the dead leaves
and you'll watch me climb again to snap
the final twists of brittle tendril.

At full stretch I shall prise them loose
then feed them down through the bare branches.
And you, my boy, will look up to me with impatience
like a climber at the bottom waiting for ropes.

Worm

The slow-worm I found
in the vortex of cuttings
is cool and still in my hand –
a sliver of mercury
a coiled spring
a silver choker laid
above the curve of a breast
that wants to be touched
and rises with breath.

Cold blood in a wire
sinuous and alive
it turns a thick whip
bulks like a hawser
at that moment
it's released from the ship
weighing its length heavily
casually through air
before creasing a white edge
through the oily water.

Could this be one of the lords of life?
I don't know.
I value though the cool line
printed across my palm
and place this poor snake gently
in a tangle of ivy and privet
near the crumbling wall
out of harm.
For there are cats
and crows to claw the scales
from its length and we need
such things by
us in the final house

– attending spirits
an amulet
a charm.

from WALK DOWN A
WELSH WIND

Late Son

Past fifty and greying, his pace
Accommodates the worrying of the day.
Always in tune with the turning clay,
He is, now, carried in the drift of seasons;
With acceptance of the first flashing swallow,
Attention to the timing of the arctic thrush.

This son, coming late, has dictated new ways:
His books piled neatly out of reach,
Doors closed carefully behind, a fuss
Made of stacking away fork, spade and brush.
During the day their television stares blindly
Into the corner, for its own safety.

Driving through the autumn back-lanes
On our way to school these pale mornings,
His eyes catch first the stirring of light
Angling tree-shadows across the Cheshire plain,
Are wise to the pools and pocked holes
Of the bruised and winding village roads.

Though there is much I can learn
From his older head, of history I had
Half absorbed; wages, depression, union-reform,
These are but a procession of his words
And our morning raw conversations return
To the welcome inconveniences of his son again.

from ALBUM

The Watchers

You are there
we can depend on you.
Speck on the screen,
white fly inching towards
the centre of the scanner.
And up above our warning station,
out over white clouds
over the grey fishing waters
your reality is a silver-glinting
massive hulk, four propellors flickering,
leisurely screwing.

A rear gunner waves
to the pilot of the Lightning:
a civilised greeting
in the blue whispering sky.

So factory worker, mid-shift,
housewife stretching shirts
up to the line,
miner scratching
in the guts of the land,
smile, you are appreciated.
The high silver Bear visits you
like a kind old uncle insisting
he immortalises the moment
in the eye of his box "Brownie".

Killing Whales

Eye sharpening down the line of the cannon:
The crack of the shot
                    high whine
Aching seconds of rope
Spiralling out of the basket.

Slack rope
           and the second, muffled explosion
Tears through bone and blubber.

Whale-back island rising from the deep.
Blow-hole like steam from a boiler.
Wild plunging
              then rising
Resigned to the ship's tether.

Belly over in a slow-motion twist
That could be the discomfort of an itch;
Until that last, low spouting
Like brown water draining a rusty cistern.

Grapple, winch the carcass up the slope:
Out of its element the mass is grotesque.

        Slice
Through the blubber to the red, hot meat.

In the ship's belly white flashes
Pattern the darkness of a sonar screen.

Circling the fleet, whales sing deeply,
Love to the hulls of factory ships.

The Circus Left

On Sunday the circus left.
Clowns became men again and drove away
lorries, cars, caravans of families;
tigers were tucked into cages
the tightrope fell
                    to the ground
a dead snake.

The big top folded into clever sections
and was handled by the dark strong men
like a tablecloth;
the four poles were last down,
lowered like trees felled in slow motion.

On Monday the boys played football again
screaming across the small ground,
avoiding at first the bare, sawdusted circle
as though it were quicksand in a dream,
then kicking bravely through its fading memory.

Hayhurst Bridge

I switch off the engine as the grey,
peeling bridge begins to creak away,
swinging around from the road
on its smooth turntable. It comes to rest
parallel to the canal seeping
its brown length through the town.
Sternly authoritative wrought-iron gates
bar the road from its gap,
as cars, lorries, a bus, queue on both sides
of the water: a man in a Rover picks up his paper;
the bus driver cups a light to his cigarette.
I get out and lean over
the cold metal of the gate to peer boyishly
at the passing vessel.
A grimy, squared-off box of a craft, out
for dredging, sends blunt waves waddling to each bank.
Below me, her men breathe smokily
up into the sharp morning air.
The gate-man emerges from his cabin
to oil, with absurd daintiness, the briefly revealed
cogs of the works. His brush strokes along the metal,
ending as the laden, low trailer of sludge
bellies its way through the gap.
                                Back
in his cabin, a flick of his hand sets the bridge
turning again, sends us scurrying to our cars
as the gates mouth apart.

                        Later,
crossing flat, open country, my nose wrinkles
at the memory of oil and river smells.
Pylons strung stiffly across the sky,
rows of trees lining the road, now mirror
the opening of the bridge-gates; renew
the certainties of straightness, crossing and entry.

Two Images From Dreams

One.

A house across the street;
bedroom window open to view
and a woman lying on a large bed,
her head crooked back to the window.
She is old: white hair matted like wool
over the pillow.
                    Below, out of focus,
the street busies itself.
The bedroom door opens,
a man enters, dressed formally.
His face is two faces:
                    one
is a moustachioed villain of Melodrama
curling a murderous smile;
the other a mourner.
His hand carries a wreath of poppies
finished with a blood-red rose at the centre.

Pause.

The woman moves:
                    her hand
stretches to the flowers
and with the weight of her whole body's arch
pulls the rose away,
falling back to the bed,
arm out rigidly over the window ledge.
Her hand, enormous, opens like a spring trap.
The rose balances at the height,
thorn hooked to the palm;
slowly, loose petals detach themselves
and fall, like drops of blood,
to the street.

Two.

A man is locking the large, heavy door
of a high-roofed hall.
An impression of neatness:
he is, possibly, an attendant, curator.
The centre of the door, at the point
where its diagonal bars cross,
dissolves into a camera-hole
through which I pass.
Inside, the skeletons of prehistoric beasts
loom hugely on spindle-legs.
Shadows move in abstract on the back wall,
and caged in the ribs of a dinosaur
a bird flutters wildly,
cutting and flapping at the bars
of the ancient guts.
A man is locking the large, heavy door
of a high-roofed hall:
an impression of neatness.

After The Crash

It was a shock to find him alive:
thirty-two days after the blizzard
had locked its ice jaws
on the lake; stilled and stiffened
the huge trees.

The dark smudge of the wreck
planted, fragments arranged,
in an immensity of whiteness:
the drama of discovery
in brittle, movie-set snow.

When he shouted, when he moved,
a shock: we sensed snow mirage.
His eyes, two prisoners staring
through the glass of the crushed cockpit:
an unexpected life regained
is a snow-birth.

But oh, in that wreckage!
The Eskimo woman and her boy
hard in a frozen embrace;
the nurse's bloody clothes
and the missing flesh.

Something has been affirmed:
after the lichen, the chewed moss,
after the desperate mouthfuls of snow,
he broke through the white seduction,
the hopelessness.
Slumped over shattered legs
he took flesh.

Crowds parting;
the white glare of the flash-bulbs.
He rises, folds the statement he has read
for the world:
walks slowly out of camera-shot,
alone, and completely beyond us.

The Flooded Valley

Under the lake's press:
rock, bone, grasses;
the soft slime
of moss and fern;

a road plunges
into the water,
winds, traces the contours
of the depths.

Swim down its cleft,
walk the length
of the sunken river
past trees wintered by water.

What can you find?
What signs are recognised?

A fish netted by
the twisted branches
of a high pine.
Its spine flaps.

A dog-fox clamped
by its leg in a gin.
Time wearing away the snout,
baring teeth into tight grin.

A low, stone church:
fish curl around the cross,
water moves the bell
tolling the silent hours.

Enter the church,
the fish turn
expectantly
for your Word.

Neighbour's Pear Tree

Disturbed by the chatter
Of starlings gorging
From the rich, fat
Fruit, birds and pears both bursting

At the seams in a warm season,
We became aware of our neighbour's tree;
A nonentity since its springtime
Explosion of frail white.

Unpicked, these pears wasted
In our eyes. Despite noise
And clumsily-thrown sticks, pears, tasted
Vividly in the minds of the scrumping boys,

Maintained, obstinately, their hangings.
The bamboos and stones that bounced from boughs
To our garden are followed by clamberings
Wide-eyed over our wall now.

This sun-struck morning his tree is bare,
Fruit stolen or gathered,
Air doctored of sound.
We lie bathing and stare

Through the delivered branches lacing the sky.
Before the wall, bleeding gouts of flower up from the ground
Our prim row of tended gladioli
Climb strongly against the sticks I found.

Towy

Past Carmarthen
the Towy promises sea
miles before the castle of Llanstephan
or the station at Ferryside.
Sand-strips finger the river
and hold banks of heron, gulls,
parading the brief islands before
the incoming of the tide.
Pasture land
rich from the hoarding of the river
feeds cattle, slow as statues.
Time crumbles the banks
sudden away under calves;
the water floods over the field
a conquering army.
Like a clock the tide regulates life:
the hawk feeds from the sky
the same shadow of necessity;
salmon swim old, known ways to the sea.

Landscape: North Wales

There is a tree standing bare as a pencil,
Holding the eye like a cross.
There is the road like a river
And rivers like slow worms squirming
Their way round stone and root.
One must have a farmhouse
Looking tired and snail-small
Against the stirring cauldron of the mountains,
And from it slate and rock walls
Numb through stretching to hold the cold land.
Sheep are essential; never more than ten,
Suffering their way by rock, moss and weed.
Lastly (though not essential) a man
May be seen to lumber at the tree,
Pull grey, autumn-speckled trout
From the streams before the quick falls
And crop his rooted sheep that chew down
The hours, leaving berries of dung
To face the tired moving of the sun.

Landscape: North Wales (Re-considered)

I take it back –
There is a tree standing bare as a pencil!
for today at Bala there is a wonder of trees;
sun seeps through a tangle of branches,
works an alchemy of gold and bronze
against the green,
wears Summer's fern to rust.
This road leads somewhere:
past the water's slow curve,
an angler propped at the edge
outstaring the lake's patience;
on a day where winds of Eastern wars
– the tight grin aching through sand into skull –
die;
and blue-clouded Aran Benllyn
holds promise of fresh weather,
then carries the eye far out
over Aran Fawddwy to the opening West
where a jet's chalky path already reaches sea.

Trains

Trains make people talk;
as rails slice through fields
of hunched feeding rabbits,
past statuesque, unconcerned pheasants
posing copper-gold against the green
showings of corn:
as with disdaining speed they cut
through the edges of cities and the arse-end
of factories,
                through the new towns,
lines of semis seen from the wrong side.

Trains make people talk.
                        Old women
pouring the past over strangers,
each other
                dead husbands, degrees and positions,
parties, decorations,
                        meaningless
no matter how often mouthed;
the dead one's garden, his boat;
"We kept a little cottage in Wales"
nothing regains reality in the telling
and your listeners will smile sympathy back,
reciprocate with their lives and distant dead.

People can talk on trains:
capsule between poles of the familiar rooms,
the grown-up children
moving always further away.
                        Between
Manchester site and London office,
cosy home and another's illness,
words like wheels measure distances,
tumbling into the black, open mouths of tunnels.

Snapshot: Man And Bird

He poses for me at the back of the shed,
hand stretched out confidently to hold
the old bird first back from Nantes.
This pigeon bounces jerkily to the invitation,
perches knowingly on the hand.
In the left corner of the viewfinder is the loft,
green and white stripes freshly painted.
If I open my left eye the camera squint blurs
and is over-ridden by the widening garden:
potatoes flowering, a line of crisping clothes,
a ragged towel holed, through which the sky shows:
these have nothing to do with the photograph.
In the print they will no more appear than
the plump corn the pigeon kisses in his hand.

The Mystery of the Homing Pigeon

for Blundell & Son, N.W.P.F.

The mystery of the homing pigeon
is being cracked.
A professor at Cornell tracks
the birds in his twin-engined Commanchie,
asserts the dependence on sun and moon,
what ancient mariners they make;
whilst a computer at the Max Planck Institute
simulates wind, magnetic field and flight.
When I tell you, you say you don't care:
"Good lofts make good birds",
receive the applause of their wings
as they take the air.

Key Biscayne

Sand white, soft and hot,
palms bent over like sheltering arms,
shadows running sand through their fingers,
cool shade.
Sea green, warm soft surf raising white;
and farther out by miles
basking sharks lulled to quiet
by the burning sun.
An horizon ship steams
across your vision:
staring, staring, you watch it
fall over the edge of the world.

Travelling

Leaving Croesgoch, the night closes in
locking the land firm
as we drive southward home.

Past Solva, and the tight twists
of the road spiral us towards sea.

Newgate strung by phosphorescent surf,
windsong and the slush of pebbles:
rain rinsing through our headlights' mist.

Six months from this Boxing Day
and our limousine inching
away from clustered scrapers,
down the cloudbursted freeway
over the Hudson to Kennedy:
a grounded flight,
the banal limbo of a terminal wait.

Hung like waves between two points,
all our time we are travelling,
unwinding the road home,
the wipers an insistent metronome,

eyes cutting into the night
needing water and light
water and light.

THE DEERSLAYERS

The Deerslayers

from a folio of twenty-four photographs by Les Krims

'Each photograph is like a short poem or a long question.'

A delta of blood from the leaking mouth
irrigates the dented wing.
Behind you, the land is ploughed and flat. No cover.
This buck's antlers close around you like claws.

★

Nova fitted with wide racing treads;
the deer's head on a sponge across your trunk.
You pose with Les Krims's shadow
speeding through to your body.

★

You're pulling that buck
out from the back seat of your estate.
High, light clouds in a fast sky.
The tongue has slipped from the side of the mouth like an idiot's.

★

The deer stiffening across your trunk in no way matches
The Pride of the Highlands'
challenge, staring out from the left side
of the sweater she knitted you.

★

Fat man, you are a freak – like someone inflated your clothes,
your tiny hand like a girl's just touching

the tip of the antler where it forks:
God's stick for pinning snakes.

*

The hood of your Plymouth stretches like
a dirty pond in the flash-glare. Four of you
posed in the car. An extended radio aerial.
Over your heads an antlered head flies in the night.

*

Two loons: two loons with loon smiles.
Two loons with loon smiles and check shirts perched on
        the hood.
Two loons with loon smiles and check shirts perched on
        the hood
with arms around 2 cold, dead doe. In the night.

*

Stone-face of a movie G.I.
The door reveals you like some encapsulated wrong.
Wide-eyed, the buck draping your roof
testifies we use you for our killing.

*

These 3 deer – bodies slotted one to one to one
remind me of 3 trucks I shot
hooked and driven piggy-back on a road upstate N.Y.
The disaffecting image.

*

Stickers: Maine; the Maple Leaf; a prairie-schooner
over Montreal; V-map of Victoria. Such travelling,
for a bland guy picking at his fingers,
so many empty-eyed killings.

★

Wife. Never beautiful, but here he has you by the car
not knowing what to do with your hands:
trophy tied across the roof, its muzzle coming
at your left side like a lover. Death's own kiss.

★

Ladder at the back of his camper
becomes a gibbet to hang this young buck.
In baseball cap,
the Sheriff of Nottingham. K.K.K.

★

Chevrolet NT 7729 from New York –
you are turning from the lens in protest.
Her hooves are safely wrapped in polythene.
Try to run: it is a wet morning and we have you on record.

★

Joker, face square alongside the strapped head
as you pose a nice-guy smile for the camera-flash.
It is evening: kneeling on the front seat your toddler
picks her nose and calls for bed.

★

Think Trout sticker on the window. Two deer
bleed open-mouthed over the roof edge. Check shirts,
jackets; giant camouflage footprints cover the camper.
Brautigan would approve of such confusion, fusion.

★

Trunk of your Continental, a blanket folded under
the white-tailed doe as at a tame birth
(lanterns in the childhood barn).
Behind you, headlights screwing through the morning's
        haze to work.

★

Your hand holding the doe's ear open for our answer.
But after all this killing, that car
blurred with movement, bisecting the frame,
is, photographically, more interesting.

★

A large buck
nosing out of the trunk
of your Buick.
Big man, you look bored.

★

You're out of the driver's window looking
back along the side to that head
spewing blood over the fender
of a Ford by Dietrich of Williamsville.

*

Little guy coming out of your VW.
Pads so the ties don't mark your hood.
Taut across your roof the doe: her cleaned, gaping,
scraped belly is a door opening to the secret of all guts.

*

Three bodies bound together over the roof of your
       camper.
The heads wilt like flowers.
By your moustaches and the shape of your two noses
I would take you to be brothers.

*

Showman with your perky hat;
left hand forking an unlit cigarette,
right pulling the short-antlered head up
from the blood that's painted your trunk.

*

Holding up a limp head that hardly fills your palm.
From West Seneca, N.Y., in combat cap and heavy
       glasses,
you are the guy who checks the forms,
files the names of the dead.

*

You and your brother – such a likeness
into your 50's. Your grandson has the intense
determined look of a future lawyer.
Across the roof, that deer's white eye stretches to infinity.

from PREPARATIONS

Strongman

A strongman you say.
Home from work would stretch his arms
and hang his five sons from them
turning like a roundabout.
A carpenter who could punch nails
into wood with a clenched fist,
chest like a barrel with a neck
that was like holding onto a tree.

In the final hour
your hands between the sheets
to lift him to the lavatory
slipped under a frame of bones like plywood.
No trouble – he said. No trouble, Dad –
you said. And he died in the cradle of your arms.

Families

A scratching about the eaves
above the baby's room.
They are nesting so loud in our heads:
insulation chewed to swaddling
through the cold months.

It is a dirt, a life:
grafted onto us.
They will infest,
scurry through pipes, timber cracks
to the secret places.

We breathe, they squeak air.
We cook, they take spillage.
Over our loving they fuck and thrive.
Our words build walls, bridges, they travel the night.
On my knees I light a fire that warms us all.

We can't wish them away, they will see it through
until a day the baited grain bites,
shrivelling the gut in on its silent self.
I will climb with brush and pan for the stiff, dry corpses.
Four would be a good number.

From Vermont

The snow breathes and stretches the length of the tall pines.
From dawn, each second of the sun,
bunched snow wrinkles and creases, its layers
tightening around the needles and branches
until the grip closes firm on itself and the load falls free.

The trees moan inside their snow
(low like the other's dreams after love)
though there is no movement, there is no wind,
nothing to stir the sharp air but walking,
the lungs' steady pump.

Tonight when I phone the line blurs,
marking the distance between us.
You'll be in our bed before my meal is finished.
When I tell you I'm missing you,
that I need you, you smile – "I bet."

Love, listen, we are so far
along the way of one another
the hold is firm enough, warm inside cold,
and when it falls it's still wrapped
around our joined shape.

Swimming Class

Our children are learning to save themselves.
From the pool, his shouts, their splashing and cries:
frog-legs, dog-paddle, flop-dives –
they ride the water, held by our breath.
We've wrapped their modest cocks with towels,
tousled and talced them dry, cowled like monks.
Pulling the wet valves, the stale air farts out:
the floaters squash like rotten fruit.

When we have gone the instructor's smoke hangs
over the tiles. He watches his butt sizzle
in a stream of piss, wipes off the mirror's dew
and inflates his biceps and chest. Every week we push
them further to a length. The world beyond
is made by accidents. We love them and they could drown.

At the Hutterites in South Dakota

Out in Bon Homme by the river
Jake the Preacher leads the colony
steadily to God.

The Schmeiden Leut survive Moravia, Hungary
and the troops of the Tsar.
The men bow their cropped heads before the earth's Word,
the women sail back over to the kitchen with purpose.
It is the wet ending of Spring
and the farm flows mud,
slicking their boots, the hems of their black skirts.

Ben Stohle offers wine, talks of the farm,
asks about the price of hogs in Wales.
The children are lost in our castles and maps.
The sons and cousins and uncles all
work the hogs and the corn.
Their eyes are heavy-lidded, their faces
moon out from the inbreeding.

Rachel Waldner runs her hand through
the fine, shining hair pinned to her bonnet.
Her eyes are deep and cool.
She waits for the heavy young man
they will bring to her.
She will take him like the rain,
the new morning.

Storm in Vermont

We run at seven through the forest
and the finest rain into
a fresh wood smell coming sappy
and sweet along the path
where last night's lightning
has cleft a pine down its length.

Under that boiling sky
we huddled in the kitchen
and you said:
my skin feels like a cat's.
I said:
the real fear roots in our heads,
it's the insult to reason.
The randomness of the strike terrifies.

Afterwards, with the sound of rain
streaming down the glass,
we all mustered stories of other storms:
on a jetty in Maine
a man and his daughter
burned up, holding hands, each
charging the other;
how some guy's weird chemistry
drew the bolt eight times
until no-one would give him work,
no-one wanted him near.

I hold back and stop. Walk
to the tree and lean my weight against it.
This pine had earthed the whole shock.

Red ants storm over the gashed wood, my hands.
I think of blood let from the flesh.
You've gone on. The pace is telling, still
my breathing jerks the air in and out.

Carnival

There is always
the Mayor's Daimler,
middle-aged belly dancers from Rotary
rippling the wrinkled folds of their paradise,
rugby forwards in knickers and tights
and then come the jazz bands –
all gaudy uniforms like chocolate cream soldiers.
The Blue Royals, Ambassadors, Crusaders,
Imperials, Majors and Coronets,
comb and paper marches from the girls' kazoos
and the scratching rhythm of the side-drums
bringing their white plimsolls down with a snap
that's almost unison.
The drum-major is boss,
her knees snapping up and the mace
swung around, flicked from side to side,
hand to hand in a semaphore of importance.

When I was a kid it was always
the rough boys from the Sec. Mod. who marched
with the cadets in the summer carnival.
And in November at the Memorial
in front of the hospital they'd have drums and rifles
while I'd wear the poppy Gran bought.
The big men of the town and the crach-ach,
the faltering, hollow bugle's lament
and the minute's silence made me feel
a crying lump in the throat.

I remember the heavy webbing and gaiters,
the rough khaki, and one year
Tich Elias coughing himself red during the silence.
In '74 he spilled his guts
in a Derry bar.

Twenty years on,
I hold up my son for a view.
He wants a soldier's bright hat,
a jazz band kazoo.
The girls march past with contest medals
over their puffed breasts.
A fat boy with spots bangs the big drum.
Sewn into the epaulet on each right shoulder
a neat pair of magician's gloves
white and skeletal.

Pwllcrochan

I spent weeks down here:
Spring and Autumn planting and picking,
thick wedges of bread and tea,
hands smelling of earth and potato juice;
story-book childhood weekends of stolen
apples, blown birds' eggs, trespassing;
rainy evenings exploring the smugglers' cellar,
shadows jerked alive by the throbbing light generator.

The Old Rectory has gone –
scraped flat for a Texaco car-park,
abandoned after six months.
Now, outbuildings enclose a grassy space,
an ache of absence.
Down the rutted lane to the bay:
from the narrow, stone bridge inland
the refinery spreads its shining tentacles,
its waste-burner roaring, glowing through the day.

The small bay is thick with reeds, wiry grass:
stream trickling over wellington-hungry mud
to slide beneath shells and sandstone shale
into the once-secret Haven.
Across the deep water from our fishing rocks
the gantries suckle from fat tankers,
steel arteries pulse away through the hills.

Looking back up to the road
I frame you in the camera lens,
centred by the cleft of the sloping fields.
You turn, Gareth smiles in your arms
and the photo worked perfectly,
bringing you into focus
and leaving all the rest behind.

As we walk back to the car, stepping from
bank to tussock, the marks of our weight in the mud stay,
draw an ooze of oil to rainbow our way.

The Spirit of the Place

Find me in the grass.

Find me in the West Wind.

I am between beats of the waves.
Winters I sleep in the seed potatoes
stocked in the dark.

Spring my sap works through tubers
stretching for light. Earth closes on me like a coat.

My engine coughs across the morning-grey farm.

I flower in the straight furrows of the angled steep fields.

I walk the coast path witnessing sun-rise
and fall of globes.

I am the flashing tinsel greed of sky mackerel,
the grey moving of tope deeply beyond Caldey.

I come blackly as cormorant.

With rain I will sweep the litter, rust the cans,
I will take buckets of brine and sluice the piss-smell
from the chapel of St Govan.
I will erase the last scratch of writing,
save that in sand.

My weather eats the oiled guns of Castlemartin.

My surf rides in white, fucks fissures and cave.

I spread my legs in the cliff heather
move with waves.
My cries crack the headland's concrete bunkers,
spike the last war's ghost barrels.

Summers I twist lanes into blindnesses of faith.
I grit through carburettors till they phlegm to a stop;
my nails slough caravans into ditches.

I turn signs.

I rustle the paper bag dropped in the rabbit warren.

Autumn my dusk stirs mice through gaps;
they lodge in the galleries' ledgers,
shred and nest in the gift shops' trash.

I am the last revolution of the screws
of the last tanker nosing into the Haven;
I hang from the Cleddau Bridge,
stare out to the disappearing sea.
I scupper the moth-ball fleet.

My hands dip into rock-pools. Cool.
Anemones flower and close at my touch.

Nights I breathe Calor Gas.

Gulls are my envoys:
they glide and sweep above your heads,
they feed on your droppings.

There! See! And then!

What have you to say?

Letter from John

It was not for want of think
that I did not rite you a love letter sooner
and this cause I think of you every hour of the day
and every day of the year
and I do love your father to cause he did lend you the horse
and cart to brought me to the train on Monday.
I shall never forget to remember what you did tell
me when coming in the cart. Oh! Mary Jane
stick to your promise won't you my dear.

I did rive Pontyprydd safe and sound
and I did go strait to the Shop
and when the master did see me he did say
"Man from where are you?"
And I told him that I was John from Maenclochog
coming to work in his shop. Then he nowed me in a minit.

Look you my work is selling cotten
and tapes and hundreds of other things.
They do all call it Happy Compartment
or something, but indeed to goodness
it was not very happy at all to be here without you,
the girl I do love better than nobody
(for all the time I am thinking of you)

Oh, yes you will ask my mother to send my watch
if it is working
cause it will be very handy for me in the morning
to know what o'clock it is.
She do know my directions.

There is a lot of girls in this shop
but not one to match you Mary Jane.
How long you are going to stop

in Mrs. Jones' again, Mary Jane,
cause I will try and get you a job at Pontyprydd
to be a Millander.
I will hask Mr. Thomas the draper about a position for you
for they say he do give very good vittels to his clerks.
It will be better by half for you to come
to Pontypridd cause then we will be near to one another
for the forehead of Mrs. Thomas' shop
and the forehead of our shop
be quite close to one another
and by and by we will marry
is it not my dear?

They say that shop girls do not make good wifes
but you know what Mr. Evans the schoolmaster said:
"Put a nose wherever you like
and it will be a nose
and put a donkey wherever you like
and it will be a donkey."
And like that you are Mary my dear.
I believe shop girls will make good wifes
if they have a chance.

Well, I will not rite you a bigger this time
for if it was twice bigger I could never
tell you how I love you.

I send you a piece of Poultry
I did make last night
and if you have not received it
send back at once.

I must finish cause I can hear somebody
asking for hooks and eyes
and your loving John must go forward.

Poultry (Poetry)

Oh Mary Jane my darling
I love you in my heart
I told you so last monday
When coming in the cart

Suppose the horse did understand
What I to you did say
I have no doubt my darling
It would have runned away.

I'll always love you Mary Jane
And you be true to me
Come up soon to Pontyprydd
To sell some Drapery.

Davies and his Daughters

You, David Davies of Llandinam,
carved your way from farmland sawmill to fame.
Locomotives steamed out of the valleys
down your tracks to the sea.
Coal hewed and muscled out of the hills
rolled its way to the docks,
roared down chutes into holds,
stoked the fires of Empire.
Country boy made good,
your statue stares firmly over Barry Docks:
the basins you gouged out of marsh and sand,
the island you linked to mainland's purpose
hold banana boats, empty water and a trickle of coke.

Privileged, your girls put sweat-money to good use.
A cool evening at Gregynog:
a fresh breeze comes off the hills,
stirs the height of trees;
a blackbird's song.
Shaw stoops to take a magnolia's scent,
his beard brushes the sappy branch.
A curtain is drawn at an upstairs window:
Gustav Holst has excused himself from dinner,
moves among stars in the crisp Powys air.

Here you stand, David Davies,
dock plans in hand,
stone toes curling in stone boots,
holding firm to your pedestal,
rooted in the town's history.
In the white museum in Cardiff
Gwendoline and Margaret's bequest room
Impressionist paintings work light's alchemy;
celebrate a century's closing:

days sinking beneath waves,
Venice, Paris, the Thames.
The books they printed are bound with love,
words blocked with angular '30's wood-cuts,
Greek urn gods warring;
Jeremiah's cursing of the voluptuous flesh.
Hand-made paper between leather.

These things were built on your gritty triumphs,
an iron-clad vision,
the creaking progress of coal-trucks,
the moulding of land and sea to your profit.
Paint and poetry and print
we owe to your industry.

Here I acknowledge it:
but go no further,
skirting such neat philosophies:
Renoir and Cezanne:
miles of slicing rails, the black tips, and miners' phlegm.

Sporting/Frieze

For thirteen years that house wrapped itself snug
around me. The landscape of childhood:
the brass toasting-fork no-one ever used,
a vigilant lifeboatman, a chalk dog,
the cracks in the grate like map contours;
my dead, unknown grandfather framed, and the bellringers;
a huge box of cars and trucks and Meccano in the cwtch.
At night under the bedclothes with spies, Germans and
        Indians:

through all the Stalag tunnelings,
Tail-End Charlie night-raids over France,
our frontier cabin surrounded and ablaze, above me
the jolly pigs pranced and kicked and bowled,
sent stumps flying, bulged goal-nets.
An unbroken frieze that ran on past our moving
until Gran's late death. A month ago we rummaged junk
in that shrunk and cluttered back-room.

I wish I'd had the sense to cut and peel
a strip from the wall.
It all went under the decorator's knife,
with the faded lino, curtains and doors –
a short blaze of rubbish in the garden.
I should have brought the pigs back to this house,
hung them in a frame, behind glass in my room,
safe, and found like a poem.

Preparations

In the valley there is an order to these things:
Chapel suits and the morning shift called off.
She takes the bus to Pontypridd to buy black,
But the men alone proceed to the grave,
Neighbours, his butties, and the funeral regulars.
The women are left in the house; they bustle
Around the widow with a hushed, furious
Energy that keeps grief out of the hour.

She holds to the kitchen, concerned with sandwiches.
It is a ham-bone big as a man's arm and the meat
Folds over richly from her knife. A daughter sits
Watching butter swim in its dish before the fire.
The best china laid precisely across the new tablecloth:
They wait. They count the places over and over like a rosary.

My Father

My father is a shadow
growing from my feet.

This shadow grows from one minute
past the noon of my life
and trails me like water.

My father is mending all fifty-three of his cars.
He works in a garden shed
by the caged light of an inspection lamp.
The red glow at his lips shows constantly
small and fierce like an airliner overhead
or the startled eye of a fox.

Ash falls onto the greased parts
of the dynamo.
He hawks and spits through the door.

His hands and nails black with grease
come out from the old paint tin
he has filled with petrol.
Like rare birds they rise
their plumage glistening and sharp
spilling green and blue and silver.

Those hands that my forehead meets
briefly and shivering.
Those rough hands I run from
like the borders of a strange country.

Poem From My Father

The two who spotted her
– approaching but no closer –
come back up the beach like dogs from the waves.

I never thought you squeamish of flesh,
and though your life has been frayed and tattered
by your predilictions for the wrong choice,

you take on the indisputable fact of death,
dealing with the mess, putting on responsibility like a coat;
your second casual corpse in as many months.

She has fed the fishes
her face.
The rings of her fingers have slipped their flesh.

Belly pregnant with the blue swell of her guts.
They have sucked through her breasts
to the heart's cage.

Six weeks adrift the wrong side of living,
she is something quite other
than wife, young woman, mother.

There's an old blanket you drop over her,
a stone laid at each corner.
Sand could open and swallow her spread body's horror.

Sentry for an hour before the police,
your seventh cigarette beginning to taste;
smoke against a sky tight as a drum.

The sea offers up ourselves to ourselves.
Looking out to the grey island,
you start to hum.

Singleton

i.
Three men in clown suits
are trying to fill an elephant with water
as the T.V. show dissolves.

An aquarium bubbles life to the delicate fish
moving each in its oblivion.

We are at such a height
that out over the town the coast
unfolds a string of lights
that maps the Bay's arms
as they pincer the dark sea.

ii.
This hospital is a space-city
we shuttle to.
A thousand-lights house
in a suburb of our life.

iii.
You shuffle to the window
and point out the edge of the campus.
I spent four years there.

All that time we watched
them build this place : ninth floor, tenth floor,
Accident Ward, Cancer Ward,

loud navvies racing dumper-trucks through the mud,
cranes swinging girders in the sky,
the drone of the big mixers.

iv.
The fish slant and cruise
through the tepid water.
They pout and suck at the glass.

v.
All the people here are dying. Carcinoma
of the throat, colon, brain.

You too, are dying.
Though they pepper with radium
the grid drawn on your shaven chest,
you are dying.

At the end of the hour
you rise, aching out of the armchair.
The arc of your back gives it away:
a year, a week, a day.

vi.
These visits we kiss full-lipped.
It must be twenty-five years –
so long since we did that,
or watched each other as carefully as this,
weighing out our words.

vii.
The lift drops
like a flat stone through water.

I'm stranded.

The night air is ice at the back of my mouth.
I drive through one sour pool of light
after another.

My Father in Pembrokeshire

One of those godly days on the Headland,
gorse with the yellow coming to burst,
the tight heather and curled grasses sprung underfoot.

Such days are numbered for you,
we spend our time here like wages.
Precious the slow, awkward breathing,
the laboured talk is precious.

The sand over on Caldey never seemed so bright,
the island stretching empty arms to the west
in that early summer Sunday
before the trade fills the streets and the beaches,
and the noise of the day washes
out from the town a mile or more,
louder than sea.

I have to go further down.
I have to go down to the water.
The way is worn rough and safe;
I crawl to the edge of a chimney shaft.
The sea lies calm as well-water,
green with rocks growing patterns underneath.

To lose myself in the long moment,
drinking in the depth, the abstract shapes.

Back at the top, you say –
Feel my neck –
and the growths blossom along your throat
under my fingers.

Under the sun, the prodigal sky,
there are no healing waters.

To My Father

Bellringing was another
of the things you didn't teach me.

How many crooked ladders did we climb?
How many belfries did we crouch in?
The musty smell of the years in the wood beams,
the giant domes balanced to move
against a man's pull.
Stories of jammed trapdoors and madness
in the deafening that draws blood.
Once you rang for the Queen
and I watched
all that pomp ooze into the cold stone of the cathedral.

I wanted to take the smooth grip of a rope
and lean my weight into it.
I wanted timing.
I wanted you to teach me
to teach my son's son.

Turning your back on that
brings our line down. What
have you left me? What sense
of the past? I could have lost myself in the mosaic
of Grandsires, Trebles and Bobs,
moved to that clipped calling of the changes.

I know now the churchbells' coming over the folded
town's Sunday sleep carries me close to tears,
the noise of worship and weddings and death
rolling out
filling the hollow of my throat.

Riverside Church

for Kate Williams

A January morning you showed me Riverside's
gothic sprawl on the West Side,
its chapels and meeting rooms;
room for all the gods we'd care to dream up.
Rockefeller's feudal big gesture
wrapped around Epstein's shining Christ.

The carillon's English bells are cold, hung
huge and grim above the length of the tower.
I'm sapped by yesterday's flight and this climb:
so tired I can't work towards the image
of my father's death the place confronts me with.
I turn away from the moment, and it passes.

The Hudson drifts slowly under thick ice,
the air knifing through to us at this height.
I see the long stretch of Manhattan,
mapped out in a frozen grid and remember
it is an island. All that energy held,
all those marooned souls.

Return to the Headland

There seems no point in angels
or ogres. Now I have no need
for the cartoons of guilt or shame.
The dead go where we send them.
At the crematorium I read 'Do Not Go Gentle'
before the vicar's book freed
your soul or whatever it be that soars
from the husk of flesh.
The curtains purred to their close.
Outside, the long summer of rain,
grey and grey and grey blurred
over Narberth's sodden hills.

It would be easy to construct a myth.
The box jammed under
the baby-seat in the back of the car,
bumping our way up to the Headland.
Early evening. The sea green and flat,
moving and murmuring in the hollows beneath
our feet. Not a cloud shaped, though the horizon
cast across Wales is dimming into grey.
The urn is some sort of alloy
like a child's toy, light and wrapped around
what we're told are your ashes.

Not in the sea – says my mother –
he was never a man for the sea –
I step off the path to the slope of rocks
and two rabbits break for cover
from the startled grass.
The stuff shakes out and falls free:
dust, ash on the stones, my shoes.
Stiff-armed, I send the empty tin
over the edge right down to the water.

A jet chalks its line high above the ocean,
pushing steadily away from night.
We turn our backs on a sky that goes on for ever.

Poem for John Tripp

We have filled this church, like a cold, damp barn
perched above Lancashire mills on the edge of the moors.
Wind that razors through to the bones;
leavings of snow on the hills,
moulded to the underside of low stone walls.

With god-knows what light, the pre-Raphaelite
stained glass records the Whitworth's son and wife:
In Loving Memory – 27 years – 31 years. 1894.
Today is Barbara in her box,
chrysanthemums, the death flowers, arranged on the lid.

Our third funeral within a year –
this friend dead at thirty-two,
her daughters too young to know what it is they feel,
like an unseen draught chilling their dreams.
I've had enough of this coldness, of loss.

John, we are under the weight of this thing
And we wol sleen this false traytour Deeth
clench the fist around the pen, we riotoures three:
you and I and the third – our dead friends and fathers,
on the road, at the desk, looking over our shoulders.

The Weather Vane

The wind is rising:
the plastic man turns his handle
and the paddles go over and over.
A trick of the eye.
The paddles turn the man,
the wind animates him.

An evening in September: light
blue and brown streaking the West sky.
The vane's tail-fin catches and spins
the whole thing on its pivot.
So the man bends and works, spins
to hold in the trough of the wind.
Dad, it was you painted the post
and fixed it firm. Last year.
That same wind moves your ashes tonight in the sea
and the grass in Pembrokeshire.

In the summer I saw the whole stretch of our coast
from thirty five thousand feet.
Flat Holm to Pennar and not a cloud.
South Wales spread out like a school atlas,
so green and small before the hours of ocean.
It was like looking back on our lives.

The last light's fallen away.
There's no man or paddles or wishing well.
You and I separated now by a long year,
going our ways into the second winter.

from LETTING GO

Letting Go

The trees shake their snow
like a dog at your window.

The world is plant and animal –
it melts, it dies, it falls.

So we make of it art.
Those dry brown grasses in the snow:

the summer's Queen Anne's lace,
old women laying their bones against white sheets.

That gust of wind, the hand
lifts snow dust from the pines.

It powders across the field, turns to
breath in the air. Something to do

with letting go.

Tannenbaum

Wooden strawberries, tinsel pythons,
plastic icicles with shepherd's crook hooks,
the toilet roll angel from school
– we amass the stuff of celebration.

I screw the tree
hard into its base and each
turn skews it further from the true
upright. Year by year

we dress the tree, finger
the strings of lights,
touching every brittle stamen,
telling the rosary of the snapped elements.

It never works, never the first time.
There's always something loose,
something to curse at.
A star falls, needles rain onto the carpet.

In the late summer the children
discover its skeleton in the hedge.
On our bonfire it crackles and spits,
breaks down to a snowy white ash.

Staring into the flames
I think of Christmas,
my mother visiting us,
using my study as her bedroom.

On my desk she lays a bracelet,
three rings, a watch and the pendant
that holds my father's face.
Gold, silver, all the things that melt.

Crane-flies

for Gareth

The foghorns keening in the bay
belie those sultry days.
September's Indian summer:
our apple-tree's grown sweeter than ever,
hazelnuts ripen and brown,
there's a morning haze across the lawn.

This year so many crane-flies
– Daddy-long-legs –
each room in our house has a pair.
They whirr and tick, crucify
themselves in high corners, against lamps.

Yesterday you came from school hurt
that boys were pulling wings apart,
snapping flies' legs like twigs
until you threatened them with worse.
"Crane-flies," you told me,
"the proper name is crane-flies."
Your anger was wonderful,
I could have squeezed you till you cried.

All the week the t.v. has brought us
the Phalange massacres in Beirut –
mangled corpses parcelled in sheets.
"Goyim murders goyim, and they hang the Jew!"
Words, gunfire: the tangled lies of hate:
this will be called The September Slaughter.
It will blur into Middle East History.
I would not expect you to distinguish it
from all the other crimes even if you should
some day read it in a book.

Except maybe the word "September"
will set your hands fidgeting
and then you'll think of crane-flies,
drawn to our lights to die. Remember
how you caught them, held each one
beating in your cupped hands,
learning that sense of life
as a distant, other thing
that would fly if we gave it wing.

The Infants' Christmas Concert

A moment of hush, held breath –
the fairies and robbers, the soldiers
and dancers are in position
– then the piano begins.
This sounds otherworldly,
each note a drop of water falling distantly.

Angels swallow trumpets,
a robot trips and turtles in his cardboard shell;
the ballerina crumples and cries.
They may not know why, but still
perform for us the pattern of sentiment,
superstition and love: we sigh,
smile, laugh and applaud.

"The Rich Man gave them a bag of gold
and everyone cheered on the day
the church had a new bell."
The couple are starched in best white –
as the singing swells, they marry
and claim their gold.
It is intensely sad and fleetingly
realises the ghosts of our innocence.

Flashlights – the year's frozen
for this instant.
Keep that – don't move – stay there,
stay somewhere like that for ever.

It all builds to The Nativity:
Joseph, Mary and the three glittering Kings
change without age, time after time.
Only the baby Jesus doll remains,

a scarred and worn wooden face held magically
fresh each year in the laundered swaddling.
The audience – parents and children in arms,
grandparents and neighbours, point and giggle,
there's a glow and, finally, we all sing.

This has worked some sort of renewal,
some sort of ending.

The Honeymoon Capital of the World

Married in New Orleans,
Napoleon's younger brother rode
by coach all the way to Niagara
and that started it.

Miles of motels to choose –
each one a pair of arms embracing
the swimming pool and parked cars.
Low lights, shower and colour t.v.
On application, you can take back home
a honeymoon certificate.

Odds are the weekend will work –
who could get bored with Tussaud's,
the side-shows, grottos, dolphins
and the biggest ferris wheel in the world?

Just down-river from the Falls
the Niagara is murky with effluence.
All that food and seed and blood –
tears of love and the wonderful moment
tears of hurt and silence and misunderstanding.

At the top of the Horseshoe Falls
hold hands, go close to the edge –
the river runs fast and smooth like
silk pulled taut, or oysters slipped
greedily, endlessly into the mouth.
Everything turns white, rises and hangs
in the air as a cold mist.
Above the water, daily, leaps
the full, clear arch of a rainbow
you could almost touch.

Affairs

I

We write fictions of ourselves.

You lining up the twenty tablets,
the bottle of gin.
Your sons upstairs
left sleeping through the hot afternoon.
While, at the other end of the line,
the woman at the Samaritans – professional calm,
killing time, pulling you back.

What was she telling you that you didn't know?
Twenty tablets counted out like the lies you told him.
And for a year you have given what is real
to another man.

I see you in the back of his car
fumbling with the straps of the baby seat;
your legs lifting off some bed of leaves
a mile from your house.
The cerebral craft of it all,
the timing of each deceit.
Not the guilt, but the mess of the thing.

And I say now –
        let it happen, whatever will.

Let your loves unravel themselves from you
to point along some path.
What you'd taken had to be given.
At the end we read the fiction of ourselves.

We go into flames with the memory of seed on our thighs.

II

You decide to tell him
and I'm the diplomat
driving off with the kids
full of false jollity,
sharing in the acts and lies.

On the beach-front
I treat them to the season's last ice-creams.
The funfair wrings its final screams of pleasure;
fat gulls hunch their shoulders into the long months
and we perch like three monkeys on the chill bench.

The ices are whipped and soft and the wind laps
the white stuff over and onto their clothes.
Out in the channel a dismal coaster steams by.
And back there you are telling him, red-eyed,
blurting it out like water dammed back and released.

I hold each child up in turn to the hinged telescope,
as we scour the grey sea.
They're unsure which eye to press, which to close:
my naked eyes fix on the other coast
for a light or a signal we couldn't lose.

Five Andrew Wyeth Poems

1. At the Royal Academy

How close can we get?
A German tourist in front of me
leans over the rope to Wyeth's
Witching Hour
The world swings from its hook.

He stretches as if to touch the canvas.
His fingers dance around
the six chairs then rise
to the blown candelabra's
guttering smoke and flames.
They instantly clench like burnt moths.

His hand returns to his side,
spreads and wipes itself down his trouser leg.

2. Spring Fed

the stone basin
fills and fills
from the swivel tap's
trickle.

The hills have shed
so much snow
and now,
the first brown grasses
clear of it,
the heifers push
up into the fields
to take the early shoots.

And it comes
again
the whole slow
turning of the season –
the softer touch of air,
the shine on the bucket,
the unclenching of things,
the lapping of the water
in the stone basin
up to the rim,
and the very first,
this
delicious overspilling
onto our boots.

3. Pine Baron

The spiky swift gestures
of an avenue of pines
and under them, this still-life:

the helmet Karl Kuerner wore on the Marne,
a sniper decorated by the Crown Prince.
Here his wife Anna uses it as a scuttle

loaded with dry cones to start her fires.
It is part of their farm now,
like a bucket or a cooking pot.

But what brings my jeep
jamming to a halt
right by that helmet on its brown blanket of needles

are the pitchy ridges of the cones,
with the sheen of oiled feathers, the curve of ears.
– They burn like a dream - she says.

4. Chambered Nautilus

Becalmed in her bed,
her face turned shining towards
the twelve panes of her window,
hands clenched around her knees,
she rides the big four-poster under the full canopy,
a sailing ship lulled
in crossing the twelve oceans.

She has a basket of papers, and light.
She has the pearl conch, a full, fluted ear
where the salt water breaks over and over,
the tides pull and run
anytime she needs them to.

And she does not have to wait long
for it is happening, the stir of water,
the wind's pulse.
And it is ready
her ship, her bed, her ark.

5. Winter 1946

The hill is in breath
like the flank of an animal.
Beyond, the fields of wintery grass,
a spiked hedge that roots
to the actual.

Along the fence-line
grooves of late snow
are crossed with slant shadows.
The air is brittle,
rare and thin in your lungs.

You appear as a wartime flier
in buttoned corduroy coat
walking away from his crash;
under the flaps of your winter helmet
your face pale as egg-shell.

Weight forward and to your right,
you are about to run down the hill
into the known future.
Your shadow trails like smoke,
your hand flapping in the air.

★

And my feeling of being disconnected from everything.
Over the other side of that hill
was where my father was killed
and I was sick I'd never painted him.
The hill became a portrait of him.

That Last Evening

you stayed on late into the night –
repairs in the workshop,
fixing the parts,
what you'd always done best.

Sat hunched over the bench
with the crescent ache of the lung wound
bending you into yourself,
you count the tools back into the rack.

In the morning you'd be gone,
the flesh globing to your skull,
lips strung tight from the swollen gums.
A streak of shit on your pyjamas.

Driving home that night,
the last time you would see the ocean
and still no closer to knowing
what engineered the waves,

why those curls of surf
rise and topple on the beach.
Imagine being unhorsed by
the clumsy arc of a peasant's scythe.

My Grandmother's Cactus

This cactus is shooting points out
from the desk at the centre of my room.
I bought it for you in the Fifties,
a kid's odd present from the Royal Welsh Show.

Gran, you grew as prickly as the plant,
had feuds with neighbours and family,
were confused by quarrels and gossip.
Now that dumb plant's outlasted you.

This year it thrives under the sun-facing window.
All that time on your window-sill held it back,
stunted by the lack of sun
through your half-drawn curtains.

In twenty years it flowered twice –
pink delicate flowers like anemones
nestling in the clumps of needles.
And sometimes the arms would canker and darken.

With the bad cut away it grew out
wide and angled crazily from the trunk.
Time after time, when I'm sunk in work
and stretch for a book, I'm spiked.

The needles stab through shirts and
wool and cloth. The jabs hook under the skin
and days later inflame as spots that weep poison.
I should move it. I should throw it out.

But Gran, it's part of you in my life.
One day I will, in turning to the shelf,
thinking of quite different things,
put my face right into it – that sure pain.

Generosity

My great uncle Charlie
known to be a generous man
ran the length of the platform
to wish my honeymooning parents well –
"If you need any money ..."
he shouted, but the words were lost in steam,
his run stopped short before he fell.

My father carried away the story as a gift:
Charlie framed in the window of the carriage,
generous in his words, humour in the grand
manner, blessing their marriage.
Like Napoleon's, his hand
glued to the wallet they all supposed
nested in his pocket
under those layers of winter clothes.

The Freezer

When they finally broke in
the place smelled like Pompeii –
dust, ash, fall-out inches thick.
She was sitting there, a queen propped
up in bed and not looking so hot.

In the garage an A.C.
road racer from the '30s worth thousands –
quality coachwork under the dust, and not a scratch.

All types of fungi in the kitchen
but the freezer was stocked and neat –
twenty-nine stiff cats packed and labelled:
"Roland" – "Katherine" – "Veronique" –
and so on, reading like a list of social
acquaintances. Curled, stretched, flat or sprung,
as if the shape gave each one a character.

The next evening, mackerel-eyed, fur
stuck like old pasting brushes,
they got shovelled into the garden.

The green eye of the freezer glowed,
the frosted chest purred and shuddered
in the empty house
until they cut off the mains.

Veteran: South Dakota 1978

If you were in demolition
taking out the bridges
as the marines fell back.
If you were ordered to cut down
the women and kids,
leave everything dead.
If you swung round like
the workings of a clock
and scythed the three officers instead,
fragged them good –
if all that's true,
then I'm with you.

But if saying this is your trick,
your way of living
with the fact you'd really
killed those peasants
(given the war and the VC
and not knowing
one gook from another
and it's making a better story that way)
then this party is flaking off
from your head like used skin
and I'm far from home
and reason and the neat confusions
that make poetry.

Trials

I believe nothing of this.
Nothing.

Lies infest these proceedings like lice
– a court of blind revenge.
You talk to me of gas chambers
– show me them.
Photographs – faked.
A man in Dusseldorf wrote me –
Ah! You don't listen.

Hermine – she is my wife.
A loving wife since the time she came
to the United States of America.
She is a citizen these long years.
Like me – an American.
How should I believe these lies?
Revenge and emotion runs wild in there
– even in the public gallery a jew
dressed in the striped-pyjama camp things.

She worked in the office I tell you
– files, typing, numbers and lists.

So how could there be justice?

Ach – they say eight hundred and twenty
thousand pairs of shoes.
Jewelry, teeth, gold teeth,
a mountain of wedding rings. Where?
Show me these things – the proof.

Who kills children must be animals.
You believe that –
kicking them to death;

the Harvest Festival of open graves;
a german shepherd off the leash tearing
a pregnant woman apart –
all the stuff of propaganda,
horror stories of the Zionists.

Enough of this Maidanek. Let it rest.

American jews want these trials
That Wiesenthal is a crazy man.
A hunter for thirty years – he
should learn to forget.
Let them all go to Phnom Penh, Uganda, the Russians,
– let them put their scruples to the test.
All I know is that for me
it will be years more without her.
Can you understand the horror of that?

One night a blanket of snow
thick over the State of New York; the lines
down. I go with her in my dreams:
she moves ahead of me, turning
in the saddle, beckoning now
with her whip. She moves towards
the smoke rising in the trees, past
a straggling column of refugees.

Hermine, my wife, my woman,
my beautiful silver mare.

First-class in the Hold

This is a calm Channel crossing
into the dark, early morning. Two a.m.
I'm purblind, lenses out, shoes off,
dazed and falling asleep on the tilting floor.
So are hundreds more on three decks,
like some community pageant of Dante.
The corpses stir as we plough towards Cherbourg,
the last half-hour roughening up,
the ship rolling like an old lover
churning in her own space and time.

To clear my head, to shape
up for the long night's drive south,
I need a book and pull out *Life Studies* –
the Lowells of Beverly Farms and Dunbarton graveyard.
Seven decades and four thousand miles away
that Boston family's declining days
compose a poet's litany of his beginnings.
And then 'Sailing Home from Rapallo'
when the shoreline broke
into fiery flower and Lowell's
Mother travelled first-class,
her funeral casket in the hold.

Elbows at the rail,
I blink and lean out into the dark.
The air slaps like a cold towel,
lights gleam from the foreign coast.
Below, someone calls out in French.

In the car-hold, under the sour-cream lamps,
we belt ourselves safely in.
Robert Lowell, now I remember how you died –
a Manhattan yellow cab, your heart gave out.

I never met or even saw you read
but it's clear your ghost rides
in the poets that survive:
Heaney, Walcott, Dunn,
write your continuing elegy.
Unsettled spirit, I'd gladly have
you shoulder me.

I start the engine as the bow yawns open.
The only lights at the end of that tunnel
are the docks and then back streets,
muted and dull.

We crawl down the map into Brittany:
place-names realised in empty squares
the Michelin doesn't gloss.
Unlit bistros and bars
all the way down until Ploermel
where we find hot, strong coffee
and the morning's first croissants –
ordering like tourists, self-consciously,
stumbling and tasting the words.

So much of what we aim at is style:
all the while the lever presses down espresso grains
and the patron's Gaulloise jigs on his lips,
I'm holding onto half-remembered lines –
Beverly Farms to West Street to Marlborough,
and then,
Marlborough Street, West Street, Rapallo
and Dunbarton graveyard again.

Jack Watts

squints across a sprouting field,
chews at a leaf, then weighs your crop
to the nearest bag.

Soft cap down to the eyes
and what had been somebody's suit
held by baling cord;
he is pigmented with dirt
as if washing would have drained
away the year's knowledge.

The whole county waits:
in April the Pembrokeshire Earlies come
a stiff, dark green out of the ground.
Jack and his tribe pour
like Winter rats from their cottage.

Jack stops at the stile,
pushes the cap back to the perch of his head,
then walks along a row to what becomes
the centre of the field.
He delivers a potato from the earth,
soil spilling from the web of tubers,
shaking from the clumps.
He scrapes through dirt and skin;
the sweet flesh goes between his leather lips,
a nugget lodging in the jags of his teeth.

He closes his eyes on the taste –
it is the soil crumbling, the crush
of frost, the rain carried in on the sea,
the sweat of planting.

He holds the ridged sweetness to his nose,
between finger and thumb it glistens,
the rarest egg, the first
potato and the last.

Pembrokeshire Seams

Wales is a process.
Wales is an artefact which the Welsh produce.
The Welsh make and remake Wales
day by day, year by year, generation after generation
if they want to.
> *– Gwyn A. Williams*

1.

Between Wiseman's Bridge and Saundersfoot
the coast path runs into coal wagon tunnels
and entrance holes drift down
into the base of a sheer cliff.
A pair of rails points from the path's edge
to launch the memory of themselves out over the bay
in perfect alignment with the next tunnel.

The children run on round: in the dark
there are hollows the shape of a body
they press themselves into. They
burst out at us like predictable ghosts
and we chase them into the light.

On the sand strip below us
the storm has flung a crop
of rotting star-fish.

2.

Those years I lived down here,
my parents let the bungalow to English visitors
and we spent the summers in two damp caravans.

We dug the garden patch for potatoes
and the hedge-bank would crumble
with dark shale, flaky stuff on its way
down the centuries to coal.
On a high fire you could coax it
to smoulder and flame.

3.

Coal was under us all the time,
the tail of the South Wales seam
surfacing again after the sea.
Shallow, tricky minings worked by families;
the men and children bunched like rats at the levels,
the women at a windlass winching up each
basket of good anthracite with a bent back.
Faults cracked and connived at the work –

this land never saw the rape of the valleys,
though the farmers' sons, worn by the rain
and sick of the smell of the shippen,
walked east and fed the deep pits and the iron.
On day trips their children's children
made their way back, built castles on the beach.

4.

My people – the Barrahs, the Thomases
raised cattle and potatoes
on good farming land from Llangwm to Jeffreyston.
Until my great-grandfather
that night in 1908

drunk and late from Narberth market,
roaring down the dark lanes, snapped his pony's leg
and turned the trap over his neck.
Six daughters, and a renegade son away in Canada,
saw the farm sold and split.

We lose ourselves down the years.

Under the earth at Jeffreyston,
wood groans, crack of the bones' cocoon.
A name smoothed away from the slant headstone.

5.

To the north, in the next county,
cottages are put to the torch for the language,
for the idea of community.

A Range Rover coasts to the end of the lane;
shadows, murmurs, a burning bottle
clatters through mock-Georgian panes.
Rebecca rises to purify the tribe.

Not here; below the Landsker
we've been eased out of such extremes.

6.

It is a summer's day. The sea burns
against the eye.
A sky full of laughter and fat gulls.

On the boat to Caldey Island,
looking back you see the fields glint.
The windscreens on the cliff
pearl like standing water.
Deep down lanes a crop of caravans;
sites flower like clumps of nettles.

We trail our hands in the sea.
What did we imagine they would hold?
In the shock of cold they whiten
to the beauty of bones, of coral.

Land Army Photographs

How lumpy and warlike you all looked,
leaning against the back of a truck,
hair permed underneath headscarves;
in make-up, corduroys, with long woollen socks
– the uniform completed by a khaki shirt and tie.

You are posed in a harvest field:
long wooden rakes and open necks in one
of those hot wartime summers. Fifteen of you
squinting into the camera,
and the weaselly Welsh farmer, arms folded,
his cap set at an angle
that would be jaunty for anyone else.
He's sitting there in the middle, not really
knowing about Hitler, or wanting to know,
but glad to have all those girls
with their English accents and their laughs.

Mother, how young you look, hair back, dungarees,
a man's head at your shoulder.
You girls cleared scrub-land, burned gorse,
eyes weeping as the smoke blew back;
milked cows and watched pigs slaughtered.
You, who could not drive,
drove tractors with spiked metal wheels, trucks.
And once, on the Tenby to Pembroke road,
along the Ridgeway, they had you working flax.
For two days only it bloomed,
the most delicate blue flowers.
Like wading into a field of water.

I see you piling the gorse. Dried spikes
flaring into silver ferns, and smoke
twisting from the piles as the wind comes in

gusts, cool from the sea, the gulls drifting
lazily on the flow.

                    And then,
one of them, too steady, too level, becoming
a Sunderland coasting in to Milford Haven:
over Skomer, Skokholm, Rat Island, over the deep water;
and, though you do not know it, over a man
who is smoking, scraping field potatoes
for the searchlight crew's supper,
who pulls and unpeels the rabbit they have trapped,
joints and throws it into the steaming stew,
the oil-drum perched over an open fire;
the man who looks up, the man who is my father,
watching the white belly of that flying boat
cut into the Haven.

Manoeuvres on Kinder Scout

Reaching Kinder's river-bed
after a morning's trek
and the game is on.
Sheep silhouetted against the grey sky
become Apache look-outs
the boys dodge. They
follow the twisting river,
keeping low to the sandy bottom
as it drains the Kinder plateau,
running to spill at the Downfall's sheer drop.
We head South with the water
oozing between high peat walls
that block all landscape,
all escape under the blanket sky.
The boys run small risks,
soakings as they leap boulders
over the gathering force of the water.
Arrow-noises zing and zip
from their mouths into the spongy banks.

I let them whoop ahead and occupy
myself in walking. Then
turning a bend come across them
in a hushed huddle. The eldest boy, Routledge,
cups a ball of fluff in his hands.
Feet away, a hen grouse waddles back
and forth for our attention –
"I'm bigger, take me, I'm bigger."
A nursery-book sacrifice.
Routledge smiles, makes a fist to hold
her chick, helpless, brushed with beginnings
of colour. Then, like some pageant hero,
he lowers that blind ball of feathers
to the heather roots.

He turns and leads us on.
One asks, "Why ...?"
"There's some things you didn't oughta ..."
Hen and chick melt back into the scrub
before our boot-marks can fill
and fade in water.

We unpack lunch
sitting on the edge of the world.
At Kinder Downfall the peat-trickles bunch
into a tumbling rush of water
the windy uplift turns to mist
that bathes us. Light spumes off the plovers
that catch and ride the air's power.
The talking dies – we are breathless at the show.

All morning, we've crossed the plateau,
so, watered and fed now, we turn for home.
Mission complete, the schoolboy platoon
races on beyond my ken to Grindsbrook Clough.
Climbing the parapet of one more peat-gulley
I find myself alone,
the wind scouring my ears like shells,
my eyes loaded by the span of humped peat.
The world is weighed under loss.
Now, pinned to this map's one contour,
I see, stark and simple, the reality
of an absolute:
                    this levelled
table-top world spread above its two poles
– Manchester, Sheffield –
and those cities laid waste
in a terror of nuclear heat,
brick and flesh charred peat-black
in a sear of thick light.

                    Strange snows
will cover this mountain.
That history is held sure,
deep in the darkness of the peat,
deep below the jagged hulk
of a Dornier, its pilot's fist
clenched for thirty years.
That bomber, overshooting factories,
the web of searchlights, slides down
year by year to its real target.

The World

This is how it ends:

a finger slips –
two Russian subs resurrected
from the ocean
retaliate
before they drown.

California
the flat Mid-West
the Great Lakes cities
New York/Washington
– all clouds, acid air.
Europe's on fire.
The Third World eats
itself and starves.

In the far North
the Inuit
listen to their radios.
They move further North and
the North wind sweeps them clean.

This is how it ends

with the last family of Inuit
eating fallen caribou
pushing North
killing sick bears
going West.
Reaching the Bering Straits:
at the edge of the ice
a bloated seal at their feet.

And farther out floating
towards them on a floe
a man, a woman and child waving
spears.

Tortoise

They bought you a tortoise and every Autumn your father packed it away in its Winter box of straw in the house-loft. One year in the late Spring, you climbed up to find the box empty. You all searched the grimy space, finding nothing and coming down dirty as sweeps.

Years later, your mother writes that four houses further along the terrace they've found a shell in the loft. Just that. A shell, hard, perfect and whole. Inside, a shrunk ball of jelly.

The image makes you shiver for days, then it lodges in the back of your mind. To travel and come to nothing, leaving behind something shaped, hard and scoured out; an object which no longer holds or needs you, being finished, and what it was always growing towards.